PRAYERSCRIPTS
Speaking God's Word Back to Him

PROTECTION THROUGH THE BLOOD

60 DAYS OF PRAYERS FOR
LIVING UNTOUCHABLE UNDER CHRIST'S BLOOD

CYRIL OPOKU

Protection Through the Blood: 60 Days of Prayers for Living Untouchable Under Christ's Blood

Published by *Quest Publications*

ISBN: 978-1-988439-69-3

Cover design by *Quest Publications (questpublications@outlook.com)*

Unless otherwise indicated, all Scripture quotations are taken from the World English Bible WEB, which is in the public domain. For more information, visit: www.worldenglish.bible

This book is a work of devotional encouragement. It is not intended to replace biblical study, pastoral counsel, or professional therapy.

Printed in the United States of America.

First Edition: July 2025

For more books like this, visit *PrayerScripts:* https://prayerscripts.org

CONTENTS_Toc205579182

PREFACE

"When I see the blood, I will pass over you, and no plague
will be on you to destroy you."
— Exodus 12:13 WEB

The divine protection offered through the blood of Jesus is
not symbolic—it is spiritual reality. From the Passover
night in Egypt to the victorious saints in Revelation, the
blood has remained heaven's covenantal seal against destruction. It
is not merely a doctrine to believe but a weapon to apply. In this
generation of increased wickedness, confusion, and spiritual
volatility, there has never been a more urgent time to live covered,
sealed, and shielded under the blood of Jesus.

This book is a 60-day journey into that sacred covering. You will
explore the power of the blood of Jesus to protect your life, your
loved ones, your future, and even your legacy. Each day is grounded
in blood-based Scriptures—verses where divine protection is
explicitly or prophetically linked to the shed blood of Christ.
Through prophetic, Spirit-led prayers, you will lay claim to divine
insurance that no force of hell can override.

My prayer is that as you walk through this devotional prayer
journey, you will move from fear to bold faith, from vulnerability
to divine immunity, and from anxiety to spiritual confidence. The
same blood that silenced the angel of death in Egypt still speaks
over your life today. Lean in—and let the covering speak.

Let the Blood speak!

Cyril O. *(Illinois, July 2025)*

INTRODUCTION

Stand Untouchable. Live Covered.

What if I told you that you could live your life unafraid of evil—because a divine shield is already surrounding you? What if your home, your children, your business, and your destiny could be sealed off from attacks, curses, and demonic ambushes—not by luck or effort, but by covenant? That covenant is the blood of Jesus Christ.

From Genesis to Revelation, the blood of the Lamb has always been heaven's answer to earth's dangers. It marks, shields, cleanses, and speaks. It is both a sword and a shield, a seal and a covering. While many believers speak of salvation through the blood, few have been taught how to apply it daily for protection. The blood is not just for your sins; it's for your safety.

This book, *Protection Through the Blood*, is your guide to living untouchable—not in arrogance or denial of reality, but in bold, Bible-based confidence in God's covenant to protect His own. Over the next 60 days, you will pray prophetic prayers anchored in the Word. Each Scripture is carefully chosen to unveil how the blood of Jesus still stands guard over your life. These prayers are not passive—they are warfare. You will cover your home, anoint your gates, draw divine boundaries, and invoke angelic protection through faith in the blood.

Don't merely read. Declare. Don't just recite. Engage. Let every prayer be a sword in your hand and a shield around your family. You are not helpless. You are blood-covered. And that makes you untouchable.

How to Use This Book

This book is not just for reading—it's for *activation. Protection Through the Blood* is a 60-day spiritual journey designed to root you in the protective power of Jesus' blood and equip you to cover your life and family in prayer.

Here's how to get the most out of this prayer devotional:

1. **One Day, One Focus:** Each day focuses on a specific blood-based Scripture and a powerful protection theme. Don't rush. Set aside quiet time daily—morning, noon, or night—when you can read, reflect, and pray without distraction.

2. **Read the Scripture Slowly:** Each Scripture is chosen to reveal God's protective covenant through the blood. Read it aloud. Let the words saturate your heart. Speak it until it settles into your spirit.

3. **Pray the Prophetic Prayer Boldly:** These prayers are written in the first person—because they are yours. Speak them out loud with authority. Personalize each declaration for your life, family, home, and destiny. Let the Holy Spirit lead you deeper as you pray.

4. **Revisit and Reinforce:** Feel free to repeat days where you sense resistance in the spirit or areas where you need breakthrough. The blood doesn't weaken with repetition—it gets louder in the courts of heaven.

5. **Make the Blood Your Lifestyle:** Don't stop after 60 days. Let this journey reshape how you pray every day. Plead the blood

before you travel, before decisions, over your children, and over your sleep. Cover your gates and atmosphere continually. Make it your covenant default.

6. **Journal Your Victories:** Keep a prayer journal nearby. Write down breakthroughs, dreams, impressions, and any scriptures or instructions God gives as you pray. Your faith will grow as you track the tangible results of living under Christ's covering.

DAY 1

Divine Protection Through the Blood

"When I see the blood, I will pass over you. No plague will
be on you to destroy you."
—Exodus 12:13 WEB

O God of my refuge and strong defense, I stand under the eternal banner of the blood of Jesus! As You once passed over the homes of Israel, so today I declare that Your covenant blood covers me and my entire household. Let every plague, disaster, and demonic intrusion be halted at the threshold. The destroyer will not cross the line drawn by the Lamb's blood.

By faith, I mark the lintels of my life with the blood of Christ. Over my children, over my spouse, over our home and possessions—I decree divine exemption. Though chaos surrounds the nations, the blood marks us as untouchable. Our dwelling becomes holy ground, invisible to the plans of death and destruction.

Father, thank You that the blood still speaks. It cries out for mercy over judgment, for deliverance over destruction. Your covenant is unbreakable, and through Jesus, I am sealed, safe, and sheltered. I rejoice in this divine Passover—this spiritual security that no enemy can penetrate.

Let this blood shield continue night and day. I decree angelic protection, Holy Spirit fire, and divine peace in every room and every journey. In Jesus' name, Amen.

DAY 2

MARKED BY THE BLOOD AT HOME

"They shall take some of the blood and put it on the two
door posts…"
—Exodus 12:7 WEB

Heavenly Father, I stand today as a priest over my home, declaring
that the blood of Jesus marks our doorposts. As it was in Egypt, so
let it be now—our house is a house of protection because of the
precious blood. No spirit of fear, infirmity, or destruction shall cross
the boundary of Your covering.

I spiritually apply the blood to every entrance—physical and
spiritual. I apply it to our hearts, minds, and bodies. Over my
children's bedrooms, over our comings and goings, over the
foundation and roof—I decree this house belongs to the Lord. Let
the blood be our wall of fire and our canopy of peace.

Lord, we are not covered by human effort, but by divine covenant.
What You see, You honor, and where You see the blood, You deliver.
I lift my hands in faith and declare: not one life in this house will be
lost; not one destiny will be cut short. We are hidden under the
shadow of Your wings.

Thank You, Jesus, for the blood that was shed and still speaks. We
welcome Your presence and expel every darkness. Our home is a
tabernacle of glory. In Jesus' name, Amen.

DAY 3

PRESERVED FROM THE DESTROYER

"…Yahweh will pass over the door, and will not allow the
destroyer to come…"
—Exodus 12:23 WEB

Mighty Deliverer, You are the God who forbids the destroyer! You
set a blood boundary over Israel, and today I decree that the same
blood line surrounds my life, my family, and my legacy. You do not
permit destruction where the blood has been applied, and I boldly
invoke that protection now.

By the authority of Jesus' sacrifice, I cancel every plan of premature
death, disaster, and demonic ambush. The destroyer may prowl, but
he will not prevail. I declare divine interruption to every curse,
accident, disease, or snare meant to devour us. The blood is our
legal defense, and heaven enforces it.

Let every evil spirit be turned away at the sight of the blood. Let
angelic warriors surround our family gates, enforcing divine
restraint. What was sent to harm us shall pass over, and what was
aimed at us shall be reversed. I plead the blood over our vehicles,
our decisions, our relationships, and every new season.

We walk forward in holy confidence, not in fear. God has passed
over, and the enemy must pass by. Thank You for this hedge of
grace. In Jesus' name, Amen.

DAY 4

FAITH IN THE BLOOD'S POWER

"By faith he kept the Passover and the sprinkling of the blood..."
—Hebrews 11:28 WEB

Almighty God, today I rise in faith—faith in the eternal power of the blood of Jesus. Just as Moses believed and obeyed, so I too embrace the covering of the blood over my household. This is not superstition—it is covenant. This is not ritual—it is relationship.

By faith, I sprinkle the blood upon my family: over my spouse, my children, and our generations to come. I reject fear and stand in holy boldness. Let every spirit of judgment, disaster, and destruction be turned back by reason of the blood. No wrath shall come near our borders, for we live beneath the shadow of the Almighty.

Teach me to walk daily in this faith—to speak it, declare it, and enforce it. Let my home be a testimony of the power of covenant obedience. May my life honor the sacrifice of Christ as I trust in Your preserving grace.

Father, let this Passover faith ignite in my children and echo through every generation. The blood speaks louder than accusation, sin, or fear. I trust in Your word and rejoice in Your mercy. In Jesus' name, Amen.

DAY 5

LIFE FLOWS IN THE BLOOD

"...the life of the flesh is in the blood..."
—Leviticus 17:11 WEB

Lord of Life, I honor the power of the blood that was shed for me and my family. Your Word declares that life itself flows through the blood—and I decree that the life of Jesus now flows through every fiber of our being. Let sickness be driven out. Let vitality, wholeness, and divine strength be restored.

I proclaim that the blood of Jesus cancels every assignment of premature death. It renews our health, fortifies our minds, and saturates our home with vitality. I declare that no weapon formed against our bodies shall prosper. Let the blood speak healing over chronic conditions, inherited afflictions, and silent attacks.

Father, I receive the supernatural life that flows from Your Son's veins. I call it into my bloodstream, my organs, my immune system, my thoughts. I speak it over my family members—from the youngest to the oldest. Where there was weakness, let there now be strength. Where there was anxiety, let peace reign.

Jesus, thank You for the blood that gives life more abundantly. We are not under the dominion of death but under the power of life. We rise and live by that blood. In Jesus' name, Amen.

DAY 6

GRATEFUL FOR THE SHED BLOOD

"...without shedding of blood there is no remission."
—Hebrews 9:22 WEB

Righteous Judge, I come today not by my own merits but by the blood of Jesus that was shed once for all. Thank You for the sacrifice that broke the curse and silenced the wrath that once stood against me. I am no longer condemned—I am covered, cleansed, and consecrated by the blood.

That blood purchased my pardon and my peace. It brought my family into covenant, and it keeps us from destruction. I declare that by this blood, we are rescued from every cycle of sin, shame, and suffering. No judgment shall land where the blood has been applied.

Lord, I rejoice in the mercy that flows from the altar of Christ. I plead that mercy over my household, over my past, over every legal accusation in the realm of the spirit. Let that crimson stream drown every claim of the enemy.

You have made a way through sacrifice, and I say yes to it. Thank You, Jesus, for shedding Your blood for me. I will never take it lightly. I honor it. I apply it. I trust it. In Jesus' name, Amen.

DAY 7

COVERED BY THE NEW COVENANT

"This is my blood... poured out for many for the
remission of sins."
—Matthew 26:28 WEB

Covenant-Keeping God, thank You for the blood of the new
covenant that was poured out for my freedom. What the law could
not do, the blood has done. I declare that my family lives under a
better covenant—ratified not by goats or bulls, but by the Lamb of
God Himself.

I receive that covering with deep reverence. Let this blood speak
forgiveness, protection, and reconciliation over my home. Let the
terms of the new covenant—life, health, peace, and protection—
be enforced in every area of our lives. We are not vulnerable; we are
blood-covered.

Lord Jesus, as You lifted that cup at the Last Supper, You declared
the beginning of a new era. I enter into that era now. Let old curses
break. Let fear flee. Let generational bondage be uprooted by the
covenant bloodline I now belong to.

I will walk boldly as a child of this covenant. The blood has secured
my family's destiny and sealed our access to divine protection. We
rest under its banner. In Jesus' name, Amen.

DAY 8

SPARED FROM WRATH

"We will be saved from God's wrath through him."
—Romans 5:9 WEB

God of Mercy and Justice, I praise You for the cross that diverted wrath and poured out grace. You have not appointed me or my family to wrath, but to obtain salvation through Jesus Christ. I rejoice in this divine exemption—purchased by blood, sustained by love.

Let every whisper of condemnation be silenced. I am not under judgment, but under the blood. My children are not marked for disaster, but for destiny. I reject every voice that speaks doom, every scheme that predicts ruin. The blood shields us from deserved judgment and undeserved attacks.

Let the blood of Jesus speak over every court of accusation— human or spiritual. We are justified, redeemed, and declared righteous. The wrath of God has passed over us because Christ absorbed it fully. What a Savior! What a covenant!

We walk forward without fear. Your wrath is satisfied; Your mercy is extended. We live in that safety and declare it boldly. In Jesus' name, Amen.

DAY 9

Entering the Place of Refuge

"Having therefore boldness to enter… by the blood of
Jesus…"
—Hebrews 10:19 WEB

Holy Father, thank You for the blood that has torn the veil and
opened the way. I come boldly—not timidly, not shamefully, but
confidently—into Your presence. This is my refuge and strong
tower. My family is safe when we dwell in Your presence.

By the blood of Jesus, we are not strangers but sons and daughters.
We enter into safety, wisdom, and divine provision. Every time we
pray, the door is open. Every time we call, You answer. Let this
boldness rise in our hearts as a flame, burning away fear and
condemnation.

May our home be filled with Your glory. Let Your sanctuary not be
a Sunday place but a daily reality. I bring my family into the secret
place, under the shadow of the Almighty. No evil shall befall us
there. No storm can shake us there.

Thank You, Jesus, for giving us access through Your blood. We will
abide in Your courts and rest beneath Your wings. In Jesus' name,
Amen.

DAY 10

THE BLOOD SPEAKS A BETTER WORD

"...to the sprinkled blood that speaks better things..."
—Hebrews 12:24 WEB

Lord of the Covenant, I tune my ears to the voice of the blood. Where sin cries for punishment, the blood cries for mercy. Where the enemy speaks guilt, the blood declares innocence. I stand today, not on my failures, but on the unchanging word of the sprinkled blood.

Let that voice be loud in my life, my family, and my future. Silence every whisper of accusation, every word curse, every verdict of destruction. Let the blood of Jesus be our advocate, our defender, and our banner. What it speaks, heaven honors.

Thank You for this divine language—better than vengeance, better than justice, better than fear. It speaks protection, pardon, and peace. I plead it over my household today. Let its sound be heard in the courtroom of heaven and in the warfare of earth.

We will not be shaken, for the blood still speaks. And what it says, we receive: mercy, deliverance, and divine covering. In Jesus' name, Amen.

DAY 11

THE BLOOD SPEAKS PROTECTION

"...to the sprinkled blood that speaks better things..."
— Hebrews 12:24 WEB

Righteous Redeemer, I stand today under the power of the blood that speaks on my behalf. Your blood does not cry out for vengeance like Abel's, but proclaims mercy, protection, and deliverance over me and my family. I declare that no accusation, calamity, or destruction shall have the final word over our lives, for the sprinkled blood of Jesus declares a better report!

By the blood, I silence every voice of judgment, fear, or inherited destruction. Let every negative decree spoken over my household be revoked and overruled by the speaking blood of the Lamb. Father, may Your divine voice echo through the blood, cancelling every curse, breaking every agreement with harm, and surrounding us with angelic protection.

Let this better-speaking blood be a hedge around my mind, my dwelling, my loved ones, and our future. I resist the whisper of fear and stand in bold confidence that You are our Defender. The blood is speaking healing over our bodies, peace in our home, and safety in our journey.

I rest in the declaration of the blood: that I am covered, surrounded, and secure. Let it speak perpetually and powerfully over every area of my life. In Jesus' name, Amen.

DAY 12

OVERCOMING BY THE BLOOD

"They overcame him because of the Lamb's blood..."
— Revelation 12:11 WEB

Champion of Heaven, I rise today clothed in victory through the blood of the Lamb. Every plan of the enemy is overthrown, every scheme is scattered, and every attack is dismantled by the power of Jesus' shed blood. The blood has already declared that I overcome—not by might, nor by power, but by the testimony of divine redemption!

I decree that my family is not a victim of fear, loss, or destruction. We overcome sickness, sudden disaster, generational bondage, and the arrows of darkness through the blood. No force from the pit of hell can withstand the authority and covering of the crimson flow that bought our freedom.

Let the overcoming power of the blood dismantle every spiritual ambush against us. Let it rise like a banner over our heads and a wall around our gates. I plead the blood over my marriage, my children, our finances, and our travels—over every entry point of our lives.

I walk boldly knowing that we are more than conquerors because of the blood. We do not fear tomorrow, for the blood has gone ahead and secured our victory.

In Jesus' name, Amen.

DAY 13

THE BLOOD SILENCES VENGEANCE

"...the voice of your brother's blood cries..."
— Genesis 4:10 WEB

Merciful Judge of all the earth, I come under the covering of the blood that speaks louder than guilt, louder than vengeance, and louder than every cry of injustice. The blood of Jesus drowns out every voice seeking to destroy or accuse me and my family.

Where demonic accusations rise, where ancestral bloodshed cries out, where injustice tries to pass from generation to generation—I silence it now by the superior voice of Jesus' blood. Let every lingering vengeance, known and unknown, be hushed by the mercy cry of Calvary's flow.

Father, may Your courts be saturated with the sound of the blood that redeems, restores, and reconciles. I declare that the enemy has no legal ground against us, for the blood has satisfied every claim. My conscience is cleared, my lineage is purified, and my home is released from retaliation.

We dwell in peace, not punishment; in blessing, not backlash. Let this divine blood covering render every evil claim null and void, and establish a new legacy of protection and grace.

In Jesus' name, Amen.

DAY 14

SPRINKLED FOR SAFETY AND SANCTIFICATION

"...sprinkling of the blood of Jesus Christ..."
— 1 Peter 1:2 WEB

Holy Father, today I receive a fresh sprinkling of the blood of Jesus upon myself and my household. I declare that this divine application separates us from destruction and sets us apart unto You. Let the blood sanctify our minds, seal our doors, and shield every vulnerable place in our lives.

Just as the Israelites applied the blood and the plague could not enter, I now sprinkle the blood over every room, every member of my family, and every part of our journey. Let our days be marked by divine exemption, and our nights by supernatural peace.

Sanctify our thoughts, our choices, and our desires. Cleanse us from the dust of the world and guard us against the contaminations of sin, compromise, and spiritual assault. May we walk in the holiness that brings preservation and the purity that invites Your favor.

As we are sprinkled daily, we are made ready and resilient—covered in grace, saturated in mercy, and immune to the reach of the wicked one.

In Jesus' name, Amen.

DAY 15

Covenant Blood Breaks All Prisons

"...because of the blood of your covenant, I have set your
prisoners free..."
— Zechariah 9:11 WEB

Mighty Deliverer, I thank You for the blood covenant that has the
power to open prison doors and tear down demonic strongholds.
Today, by the blood, I break every invisible chain holding me and
my family captive—whether emotional, spiritual, financial, or
generational.

I invoke the terms of Your covenant, sealed by the precious blood
of Jesus. Let every confinement placed by fear, limitation, or trauma
be shattered. Where the enemy thought he had locked us in, the
covenant blood now speaks release and freedom.

I decree freedom from mental torment, from cycles of delay, from
family bondage, and from the grip of sin. By this blood covenant,
my household walks in liberty. No trap of the enemy can hold us,
for we have been set free by a superior and eternal agreement.

Let the blood covenant shout over our lives: "Free!" Let every chain
break, every door swing open, and every captive walk out into
destiny.

In Jesus' name, Amen.

DAY 16

ANCHORED IN AN ETERNAL COVENANT

"...the blood of the eternal covenant..."
— Hebrews 13:20 WEB

Eternal Father, I anchor my life and my family in the unshakable covenant sealed by the blood of Jesus. This is not a fragile agreement—this is an everlasting bond that secures us through every storm, trial, and attack of the enemy.

By this eternal covenant, I speak divine preservation over my lineage. We are not exposed to chaos or casualties. We are held in covenant safety, a safety that is not dependent on human ability but on the faithfulness of a God who cannot lie.

Let the eternal blood covering insulate us from crisis and wrap our journey in peace. I declare that no matter what shifts in the world, we are anchored by the unchanging promise of divine protection through the blood.

Because of this covenant, my children are safe, my marriage is guarded, and our destiny is preserved. We dwell in security that never expires.

In Jesus' name, Amen.

DAY 17

Washed and Kept by the Blood

"...washed us from our sins by his blood..."
— Revelation 1:5 WEB

Lamb of God, I exalt You for the cleansing power of Your blood. Not only have You washed me, but You continue to keep me. Your blood didn't just remove my past—it actively shields me from the accuser's reach and condemnation's grip.

I declare over my life and family that we are not under guilt, shame, or threat. The blood has erased our failures and sealed our future. The voice of self-condemnation is silenced, and the stain of sin is removed from our history.

By the blood, we stand accepted, defended, and protected. I plead this blood over our hearts and minds—that we remain free from fear, free from sin's power, and free from every chain that tries to reattach.

Let the blood that washed me keep me. Let it be a river that never runs dry, flowing daily over my household with grace and power.

In Jesus' name, Amen.

DAY 18

WASHED AND GUARDED IN SPIRIT

"...hearts sprinkled... bodies washed with pure water."
— Hebrews 10:22 WEB

Precious Redeemer, I receive the sanctifying touch of Your blood this day. Wash my heart, sprinkle my spirit, and let purity surround every aspect of my being. I declare that I, and my family, are vessels made holy and protected by the cleansing stream of heaven.

Let no spiritual defilement gain access to us. Let no dark imagination take root. May the water of the Word and the blood of the Lamb create a fortress around our souls. We are cleansed from the inside out and guarded against the temptations and attacks of the enemy.

Our thoughts are washed, our desires are purified, and our actions are sanctified. Let this continual cleansing set us apart, make us strong, and keep us from slipping into compromise.

We walk in spiritual cleanliness and divine defense. We live washed, sprinkled, and protected by the unrelenting love of God.

In Jesus' name, Amen.

DAY 19

BLOOD-CLEANSED AND ENEMY-PROOFED

"...cleanse your conscience... to serve the living God?"
— Hebrews 9:14 WEB

Righteous God, I thank You for the power of the blood to cleanse not only my sins, but my conscience. I declare that no guilt, torment, or false accusation shall live rent-free in my mind. The blood has gone deeper than behavior—it has cleansed my internal world.

Let every voice of shame, regret, or fear be silenced by the blood. I decree that my household shall not serve You from a place of fear, but from a place of holy boldness, joy, and love. Let the blood purge every hidden accusation and break the influence of enemy lies.

My conscience is clear. My inner world is at peace. My spirit is free to worship, to serve, and to obey. Let this cleansing guard our minds and protect our future.

We are shielded within and without—washed in truth and protected by love.

In Jesus' name, Amen.

DAY 20

Renewed in Covenant Safety

"...this is the blood of the covenant..."
— Exodus 24:8 WEB

Covenant-Keeping God, I renew my alignment today with the blood of the covenant. I do not live uncovered—I live bound to a promise sealed by sacrifice. I declare that this covenant is active over me and my family, preserving our lives and marking us for protection.

Let every danger that seeks to approach us see the sign of the covenant and turn back. Let the terms of divine safety and favor override every threat and cancel every evil expectation. This is not a human agreement—it is a heavenly bond written in blood.

I claim covenant rights of peace, defense, and divine intervention. I declare that sickness, strife, and sudden destruction are rebuked by covenant terms. My home is a blood-covered territory, and every door is marked with divine preservation.

Thank You for this covenant that cannot fail. I walk in its confidence and live in its shelter.

In Jesus' name, Amen.

DAY 21

PROTECTED FROM SICKNESS AND AFFLICTION

> "But he was pierced for our transgressions. He was crushed for our iniquities. The punishment that brought our peace was on him; and by his wounds we are healed."
> — Isaiah 53:5 WEB

O healing Redeemer, by the power of the blood of Jesus, I decree divine protection over my body and the bodies of my loved ones. Every infirmity, disease, or affliction lurking in darkness must bow to the finished work of the cross. The blood that flowed from Your wounds secures our health, and I stand in that covenant today declaring that no plague shall claim us, no diagnosis shall define us, and no symptom shall persist.

Let the healing virtue of the Lamb flow through every cell, every organ, and every system in my household. I declare supernatural immunity for my children, divine strength for my spouse, and restoration for every area of our health. We reject the grip of sickness and command its grip broken now by the blood. Let Your healing wings overshadow us daily.

Where affliction has lingered, I command the reversal now. The blood testifies louder than symptoms. It declares healing, wholeness, and divine alignment with heaven's will. I cover my family in that testimony today. No terminal word will prevail, and no generational affliction will continue. By His wounds, we are healed and preserved. In Jesus' name, Amen.

DAY 22

PURITY THAT DISARMS THE ACCUSER

"But if we walk in the light as he is in the light, we have fellowship with one another, and the blood of Jesus Christ, his Son, cleanses us from all sin."
— 1 John 1:7 WEB

Righteous Father, I run under the cleansing flow of Jesus' blood and declare that every stain of guilt, shame, or sin is washed away. Let the light of Your presence shine upon me and my family, purging every hidden defilement. We are no longer vulnerable to the accuser because the blood speaks on our behalf—it silences every claim and breaks every condemnation.

I declare our conscience is clear, our hearts purified, and our spirits renewed. We will not walk under false guilt or the manipulation of past mistakes. The enemy's access is revoked, his evidence dismissed, and his voice muted. We belong to the blood-washed, and we will not be bound again.

Every member of my household is covered. Our thoughts, our behaviors, and our decisions come under divine cleansing. May we walk in unity, accountability, and holy joy. Let the purity purchased for us manifest practically, that we live blameless and bold.

In Jesus' name, Amen.

DAY 23

COVERED BY PSALM 91 PROTECTION

"No evil shall happen to you, neither shall any plague
come near your dwelling."
— Psalm 91:10 WEB

Mighty Deliverer, I stand in the security of Your covenant,
declaring that because of the blood, Psalm 91 is not just a promise
but our daily reality. I decree that no evil will come near our
family—no harm will touch our dwelling, no plague will overtake
our health, and no terror will pierce our peace.

I activate divine protection over every room, every vehicle, and
every location we set foot on. The blood of Jesus marks our
entrances, saturates our atmosphere, and surrounds us like fire.
Angels are dispatched because the blood speaks. Destruction must
pass over.

Every evil plot, seen or unseen, collapses before it even begins.
Every arrow sent against our lives returns to the sender. The blood
is our insurance policy—unbreakable, unstoppable, and forever
effective. Under this covering, we walk confidently, we sleep
peacefully, and we live boldly.

In Jesus' name, Amen.

DAY 24

SECURED AS GOD'S PROTECTED PROPERTY

"They sang a new song, saying, 'You are worthy to take the
book and to open its seals, for you were killed, and bought
us for God with your blood…'"
— Revelation 5:9 WEB

Worthy Lamb, I lift my voice in agreement with heaven's chorus—
I am purchased, redeemed, and secured by Your blood. My life and
the lives of my family members are not up for negotiation. We are
God's property, sealed and protected from every trespassing spirit,
force, or fear.

Because You paid the ultimate price, no demon can claim legal
ground. I decree every attempt of the enemy to access our lives is
denied. We are not abandoned; we are under divine ownership.
Your mark is upon our hearts, our names are inscribed on Your
hands, and our destiny is wrapped in Your covenant.

We belong to the Most High. I declare this over my spouse, my
children, and every generation to come. Our lives are guarded, our
purposes preserved, and our steps ordered by Your Spirit. The
blood speaks redemption, and that redemption includes divine
protection.

In Jesus' name, Amen.

DAY 25

HIDDEN IN CHRIST THROUGH COMMUNION

"He who eats my flesh and drinks my blood lives in me,
and I in him."
— John 6:56 WEB

Living Bread from Heaven, I enter the sacred mystery of communion and declare that I and my household are hidden in Christ. Your blood is not just symbolic—it is active, it is powerful, and it brings union with divine life. We drink of that covenant and declare that every work of darkness is cut off from us.

By the blood, we are no longer exposed. By the blood, we live in You, and You in us. Our dwelling place is not just our home but Your presence. Every enemy that seeks to find us finds You first, and they flee. We live from the inside out, carried by Your Spirit, covered by Your life.

Let communion be our daily shield. I bless every meal as holy ground, and every remembrance of You as a wall of fire around us. My family shall not be shaken. We are saturated in divine presence, consumed by covenant, and fortified in fellowship.

In Jesus' name, Amen.

DAY 26

MERCY PREVAILS OVER JUDGMENT

"He shall take some of the blood of the bull, and sprinkle
it with his finger on the mercy seat…"
— Leviticus 16:14 WEB

Merciful Father, I thank You that the blood of Jesus now speaks
from the true mercy seat in heaven. Every judgment, every curse,
every deserved consequence has been overruled by mercy. I declare
that mercy speaks louder than the enemy's accusations. Mercy
covers my family. Mercy defends our destiny.

Let the sprinkled blood silence cycles of judgment and
condemnation. Where we've fallen short, mercy intervenes. Where
we've missed the mark, mercy restores. I call upon mercy to invade
my bloodline, break generational yokes, and cleanse patterns of
defeat.

I release mercy over our finances, our health, our decisions. I plead
the blood over every legal matter, every medical diagnosis, every
family dispute. The mercy seat is not far—it is active now. Let its
voice reverberate through every room of our home.

In Jesus' name, Amen.

DAY 27

Blood Disarms Death and Hell

"...that through death he might bring to nothing him who had the power of death..."
— Hebrews 2:14 WEB

Conquering Savior, I declare that death has lost its sting and hell its power because of Your shed blood. You did not just die—you disarmed. You did not just suffer—you shattered every force that enslaved us. I proclaim that over my life and my family: we are not captives to fear, torment, or death.

Let the authority of the blood break every agreement with the grave. I renounce premature death. I cast off fear of disaster. My home is a fortress surrounded by resurrection power. You brought the enemy to nothing, and I declare his tactics are powerless against us.

Let my family walk in the confidence of divine life. Let joy, strength, and peace flow through our days. We are blood-protected, not accident-prone. We are life-carriers, not victims of death's shadow. What You conquered, we now overcome.

In Jesus' name, Amen.

DAY 28

Victory Over Every Demonic Force

"Having stripped the principalities and the powers, he made a show of them openly, triumphing over them in it."
— Colossians 2:15 WEB

Triumphant King, I lift high the banner of Your victory. By the blood, You disarmed every principality and made a public spectacle of their defeat. Today, I align my family with that triumph. No demon, hex, or power of hell can stand against the blood-stained banner of Christ.

We are not afraid of the enemy's plots. We expose them, dismantle them, and reverse them by Your authority. I declare over my household: we are not harassed, we are not tormented, we are not afflicted. We are seated with Christ in heavenly places, covered by blood, empowered by the Spirit.

Let angels be dispatched. Let darkness be scattered. Let demonic resistance break and bow. My home is a victory zone. My children carry Your authority. My spouse walks in Your dominion. Together, we enforce the cross's victory in every room, every day.

In Jesus' name, Amen.

DAY 29

GOD IS ON OUR SIDE

"What then shall we say about these things? If God is for us, who can be against us?"
— Romans 8:31 WEB

Father of Glory, I declare that the blood of Jesus is the eternal proof that You are for us. You did not spare Your Son, and by His blood, we are marked as Yours. Who can challenge our standing? What force can oppose our peace?

I decree that no plan against my family shall prosper. We are not abandoned, we are backed by heaven. Let every fear dissolve in the revelation of Your favor. The blood says, "God is with you." I speak that over my household, our business, our future.

Every opposition must fail. Every tongue that rises in judgment is silenced. Every shadow of resistance is overcome. You are our defender, our fortress, our Father. And because of the blood, we are forever safe in Your will.

In Jesus' name, Amen.

DAY 30

ANGELIC PROTECTION ACTIVATED BY BLOOD

"The angel of Yahweh encamps around those who fear him, and delivers them."
— Psalm 34:7 WEB

Commander of the Lord's Armies, I invoke the power of Your blood to activate angelic encampments around my life and my family. We stand under Your fear and reverence, and because of the blood, divine escorts surround us night and day.

Let Your angels guard our children as they sleep, go to school, and walk in this world. Let them shield us from accidents, ambushes, and sudden calamity. I declare that no demonic tracking, no wicked plan, no hidden danger can penetrate the covering of angelic fire.

Let dreams be guarded, peace be preserved, and journeys be protected. My household is not vulnerable—we are divinely defended. Where danger lurks, let angels war. Where evil plots, let angels frustrate. The blood has summoned heaven's guard, and we walk in holy safety.

In Jesus' name, Amen.

DAY 31

MARKED FOR DIVINE PURPOSE

"You shall take some of its blood and put it on the tip of
the right ear of Aaron, and on the tip of the right ear of his
sons, and on the thumb of their right hand, and on the big
toe of their right foot."
—Exodus 29:20 WEB

Mighty God, I stand today under the covenant power of the blood
of Jesus. As one marked for divine purpose, I receive the sanctifying
touch of the blood upon every part of my being. Let the blood touch
my ears—consecrate my hearing. Let my ears be sensitive only to
Your voice. May every other sound be silenced—the noise of fear,
distraction, and the world's deception.

Let the blood sanctify my hands. All that I touch shall prosper in
righteousness. My hands shall not be instruments of harm but
healing. My labor is covered. My work is redeemed. My family's
efforts are washed in the blood of protection and purpose. No curse
shall cling to our hands.

Let the blood be upon our feet. We will not wander into
destruction. Our steps are ordered in righteousness. We tread over
serpents and scorpions. As for me and my house, we walk in paths
of peace, authority, and protection. We are sealed in the covenant
of purpose and power.

Father, we are wholly Yours—ear, hand, and foot. No part of us is
left uncovered. Let this divine marking distinguish our family in the
spirit realm. We are consecrated and kept for Your glory. In Jesus'
name, Amen.

DAY 32

BLOOD-COVERED SENSES FOR DISCERNMENT

"The priest shall take some of the blood of the trespass
offering, and the priest shall put it on the tip of the right
ear of him who is to be cleansed..."
—Leviticus 14:14 WEB

O Most Holy One, by the blood of the Lamb, I bring my family
under the divine touch of consecration. Just as the priest anointed
the ear, thumb, and toe with blood, I declare today that our spiritual
senses are blood-covered for divine discernment. No longer shall
our ears be polluted by the voices of deception.

I speak over my family's ears—may we hear heaven clearly. Let
every lie be muted, every manipulation shattered. Let the whisper
of the Holy Spirit become unmistakably clear. I declare the blood
covers our eyes to see as You see, our minds to perceive by Your
Spirit, and our hearts to respond in holiness.

Father, let this blood application go beyond symbol and become
our daily reality. We shall not touch what is unclean, nor walk
where You have not sent us. The blood is our filter—safeguarding
us from defilement and guiding us into purity.

May our children grow in discernment. May we move with holy
wisdom. Let every part of our family be consecrated through this
sprinkling of Christ's blood. In Jesus' name, Amen.

DAY 33

SEALED FROM HARM AND JUDGMENT

"Don't harm the earth, neither the sea, nor the trees, until we have sealed the bondservants of our God on their foreheads!"
—Revelation 7:3 WEB

Righteous Judge and Covenant Keeper, I declare today that my household is sealed by the blood of Jesus! We are not left to chance, uncovered in the chaos of this world. Your seal is upon our heads, our lives, our destinies. The destroying winds of judgment will not come near because we bear the mark of the blood.

Father, just as You delayed harm until Your servants were sealed, delay destruction and devastation from reaching my family. The seal of Christ's blood is upon our doors, minds, and hearts. We are hidden under the crimson mark. We are counted among the preserved.

I prophesy that calamity will pass over us. No weapon formed will prosper. We are distinguished by the eternal covenant. The same Spirit that sealed the saints of old now affirms our divine exemption. My children, my spouse, and I stand secure.

Thank You for the seal that cannot be removed, for the protection that is unshakable. We are engraved in You. Let this mark testify continually in the courts of heaven that we belong to the Lamb. In Jesus' name, Amen.

DAY 34

EXEMPT BY THE MARK OF BLOOD

"Kill utterly the old man, the young man and the virgin, and little children and women; but don't come near any man on whom is the mark."
—Ezekiel 9:6 WEB

God of Justice and Mercy, I stand as one covered by the mark of the blood. In the day of judgment and shaking, let this divine mark be evident upon my household. As destruction moves through the land, let the seal of Jesus' blood scream "EXEMPTED!" over my family.

Father, not by our righteousness but by the righteousness of Christ, we are set apart. The destroyer shall not draw near. We are not subject to the judgment of the wicked. Your mercy speaks louder than wrath. We wear the crimson mark upon our foreheads—visible in the spirit realm, unremovable, eternal.

Let every demonic force that scans for vulnerability bypass us. Let every spirit of death and violence skip our homes. We are marked for life, safety, and divine preservation. My children shall live and not die. My spouse is covered. Our household is hidden in the secret place.

This mark is covenantal. It speaks louder than accusations and protects stronger than earthly guards. We remain within Your boundaries of mercy and grace. In Jesus' name, Amen.

DAY 35

COVENANT BLOOD ESTABLISHES MY SHIELD

> "He said to him, "Bring me a heifer three years old, a female goat three years old, a ram three years old, a turtledove, and a young pigeon." He brought him all these, and divided them in the middle, and laid each half opposite the other..."
> —Genesis 15:9-10 WEB

O Covenant-Making God, You initiated a blood covenant with Abraham that speaks even today through Christ. As the pieces were laid in the ancient path of promise, so the blood of Jesus has laid down a shield around my household. We are encompassed by covenant.

This covenant is not of man, but of God. It cannot be broken, voided, or erased. Because of it, we are shielded from destruction, defended in battle, and surrounded by divine fire. The sacrifice has already been made. The blood has already spoken.

Lord, I step into the pathway of promise, just as Abraham did. I bring my family into this ancient, unbreakable bond. We walk between the pieces—between judgment and mercy—and we come out sealed by love and protection.

Let this covenant answer every attack. Let it defend us in the unseen realm. Let the God who cut covenant with blood rise to defend our home. In Jesus' name, Amen.

DAY 36

ENGRAVED IN GOD'S HANDS

"Behold, I have engraved you on the palms of my hands…"
—Isaiah 49:16 WEB

Father, how precious and powerful is Your promise! I declare today that I and my household are not forgotten, not forsaken, but engraved upon the very palms of Your hands. The blood of Jesus has written our names where no man or devil can erase them.

This engraving is not symbolic—it is covenantal. It means we are permanently remembered, perpetually protected, and eternally seen. Every time You stretch forth Your hand, You see us. Every move of Your power carries our names within it.

I rest in the knowledge that Your hands are mighty to save. My family is within Your grasp. No matter what arrows fly, what storms arise, or what chaos surrounds, Your engraved palm preserves us. You carry us close, shield us strong, and lead us sure.

Because of the blood, we are not among the forgotten. We are family to the Almighty. We are not drifting—we are held. In Jesus' name, Amen.

DAY 37

UNTOUCHABLE UNDER BLOOD PROTECTION

"I give eternal life to them. They will never perish, and no one will snatch them out of my hand."
—John 10:28 WEB

Great Shepherd, I rejoice in the eternal security found in Your hand. I speak boldly today that my family is untouchable, for we are kept in the hand of the One who never fails. The blood has sealed us in, and no force can snatch us out.

The enemy may try, but he cannot penetrate the grip of God. Death may threaten, but it cannot overrule the covenant. Because of the blood, we are covered by the hand that holds galaxies and commands angels. This hand is our home, our shield, our hiding place.

I decree that no snare, accusation, or attack will remove us from the grip of divine safety. The hand that holds us is pierced with love. The hand that saved us is strong with power. My children are in that hand. My marriage is in that hand. We rest secure.

Thank You, Jesus, for holding us. No fear shall prevail. No enemy shall succeed. We are covered in Your grasp, and we shall never be lost. In Jesus' name, Amen.

DAY 38

THE BLOOD SILENCES EVERY ACCUSER

"Who could bring a charge against God's chosen ones? It
is God who justifies."
—Romans 8:33 WEB

Justifier and Redeemer, I lift my voice today in the courtroom of
heaven. I stand covered in the blood that silences every accusation.
My family is not at the mercy of hell's opinions—we are justified by
the blood!

Every charge the enemy has formed, every curse spoken, every lie
released, is now rendered null and void. I decree: Let the blood
answer! Let the accuser be silenced! Let every generational curse be
broken, every legal ground dissolved.

We are chosen and covered. The blood testifies louder than any
voice of guilt or shame. My household is shielded from
condemnation. We are the righteousness of God in Christ. No
tongue that rises against us shall prosper.

Father, thank You that Your verdict over us is "JUSTIFIED." The
Judge of all the earth has ruled in our favor, and the blood is our
defense. In Jesus' name, Amen.

DAY 39

RENEWED COVERING BY ATONING BLOOD

"Aaron shall make atonement on its horns once in the year… with the blood of the sin offering."
—Exodus 30:10 WEB

Merciful High Priest, I thank You that atonement is not a thing of the past—it is alive today through Your eternal blood. I bring my family under the yearly renewal of covering, established forever through the Lamb.

Every cycle of evil is broken. Every unrepented sin is cleansed. Every spiritual door is closed. We are not uncovered—we are atoned for! The blood on the altar has secured perpetual protection for our household.

Father, let this divine transaction be renewed upon our lives. As Aaron anointed the altar once a year, so I plead the blood afresh over every altar in my life—family, work, worship, and destiny. Let Your mercy speak louder than our faults. Let Your grace shield us again.

We are not exposed to the devourer. The blood still works, still covers, still cries out for us. Thank You for atonement that never expires. In Jesus' name, Amen.

DAY 40

HEDGE OF PROTECTION BY THE BLOOD

"Haven't you made a hedge around him and around his house and around all that he has, on every side?"
—Job 1:10 WEB

Faithful Protector, I declare today that my household is surrounded. You have built a hedge that no enemy can breach. This is not mere favor—it is blood-wrought defense. The same hedge that covered Job now covers me, through the blood of Jesus.

Around my family, You've placed fire. Around our health, You've stationed angels. Around our property, You've drawn the line with Your crimson power. Every side is defended. No back door left open. No hidden gate exposed.

Let this hedge remain unbroken. Let no curse jump it. Let no witchcraft scale it. The blood is the boundary! The hedge is the testimony! My children play within its safety. My spouse and I labor under its shade.

Thank You for divine perimeter. Thank You for surrounding love. Thank You for the ever-working power of the blood. We dwell securely inside the hedge. In Jesus' name, Amen.

DAY 41

WALK IN STRENGTH AND WHOLENESS

"He brought them out with silver and gold. There was not one feeble person among his tribes."
— Psalm 105:37 WEB

O Lord, my Mighty Redeemer, I stand under the protection of the same covenant that brought Your people out of bondage whole, strong, and lacking nothing. By the power of Jesus' blood, I declare that weakness, disease, and infirmity have no hold over me or my household. Let the same force that raised Israel in strength now surge through every fiber of our being.

Father, I release the blood of Jesus into every cell, every system, and every function of our bodies. Let divine vitality flood our bones, energy return to our limbs, and mental clarity be restored. We shall not grow weary, and we shall not be worn down by affliction or fatigue. We walk in supernatural stamina, preserved by the covenant of strength sealed in Jesus' blood.

I decree over my family that no one among us shall be feeble. No child shall be weak, no spouse shall be downcast, no parent shall be broken. Strength is our portion and vitality our inheritance. The blood speaks power into our physical frame and sets a divine standard of wellness.

Thank You, Jesus, for making us a tribe of the unbroken and undefeated. In Jesus' name, Amen.

DAY 42

CANCEL EVERY WEAPON FORMED

"No weapon that is formed against you will prevail..."
— Isaiah 54:17 WEB

Almighty Defender, by the authority of the blood of Jesus, I dismantle every weapon that has been fashioned against me and my household. No arrow, curse, hex, or strategy of the wicked shall penetrate the covering You have placed around us. Let every plan of darkness crumble before it takes form.

I invoke the blood of Jesus as our impenetrable shield. Every spoken curse is reversed. Every spiritual attack is rendered powerless. Every demonic plot is exposed and neutralized. We stand untouched because the blood renders every weapon ineffective and every accusation void.

Let the blood nullify generational curses, break ancestral pacts, and terminate lingering assaults in the spirit. My family walks in an atmosphere where weapons disappear before impact. The blood of Jesus renders every strategy of hell null and void.

Father, You have declared our vindication comes from You, and the blood ensures our victory. Therefore, I decree: no weapon formed shall prosper today, tomorrow, or ever again. In Jesus' name, Amen.

DAY 43

GOD'S ARMY, FEARLESS AND READY

"With us is Yahweh our God to help us and to fight our battles."
— 2 Chronicles 32:8 WEB

Lord of Hosts, I rise today in the assurance that You, O Mighty Warrior, are with me. The blood of Jesus has enlisted my family into a divine battalion that cannot be outnumbered or outmatched. You help us. You fight for us. And because of that, we shall not fear.

We take our stand under the covenant of blood, fearless and fortified. I decree over my home that fear shall not paralyze, worry shall not consume, and doubt shall not reign. The sound of divine warfare echoes in our atmosphere—Yahweh is near!

Let every demonic intimidation melt before the presence of the blood. Let terror be silenced, and torment broken. I call forth holy confidence in my children, boldness in my spouse, and unwavering trust in my soul. We do not fight alone; the Lord our God is our shield and strength.

So today we march forward, not in our own strength but under the banner of divine blood protection. No enemy can stand when God is with us. In Jesus' name, Amen.

DAY 44

BLOOD ROUTES EVERY ATTACK

"Yahweh will cause your enemies who rise up against you
to be struck before you."
— Deuteronomy 28:7 WEB

Victorious God, I rise and call on the blood of Jesus to route every
enemy before they reach our gates. Let the enemy that rises up
against me and my family meet a force far greater than their own.
Let Your blood go ahead of us as a blazing defense.

Father, any attack planned in secret, launched in darkness, or
whispered by the wicked—let it be reversed. Let confusion fall
upon the enemy's camp. As the blood speaks, may every ambush be
exposed, every plot be shattered, and every advance be turned to
retreat.

I release this same protection over my children, spouse, loved ones,
and spiritual community. Let every attack—physical, emotional, or
spiritual—be deflected by the covenant blood. We shall not fear
what rises against us because what rises against us shall fall.

Thank You, Lord, for securing our every step and striking down
those who would do us harm before they ever reach us. In Jesus'
name, Amen.

DAY 45

THE BLOOD FIGHTS MY BATTLES

"Yahweh will fight for you, and you shall be still."
— Exodus 14:14 WEB

Warrior God, I lift my eyes and declare that the battle is not mine, but Yours. The blood of Jesus is my signal to the heavens that I am under divine defense. Where I have no strength to fight, Your blood speaks and wins.

Father, arise and contend with those who contend with my family. Let every force of resistance melt in the presence of Your justice. I silence the urge to strive in my own might and instead anchor myself in the blood that never fails.

Every demonic onslaught launched against our progress—be arrested now. Every war against our health, finances, and peace— be overturned by divine intervention. Let the blood of the Lamb stand between us and the fury of the enemy.

I rest in the stillness of victory already won. I shall not be moved, because the Lord Himself fights for me and my house. In Jesus' name, Amen.

DAY 46

BLOOD CRIES FOR MY JUSTICE

"They cried with a loud voice, saying, 'How long... until you judge and avenge our blood...?'"
— Revelation 6:10 WEB

Righteous Judge, I call upon the power of the blood that still speaks from the throne. Let the blood of Jesus answer every injustice, repay every wrong, and overturn every verdict spoken in darkness against me and my family.

Where there has been betrayal, bring restoration. Where harm was done in secret, bring divine justice in the open. Where our names have been slandered, our destinies tampered with, or our labor stolen, let the blood cry out until heaven moves in our favor.

Father, I stand under the covenant that demands righteousness. The blood of Jesus doesn't cry out for revenge—it cries out for divine justice. Let it speak against premature death, false accusation, and unrighteous loss.

Because of the blood, I declare that we shall be vindicated, recompensed, and restored. Let justice flow like a river into every area where we've been wronged. In Jesus' name, Amen.

DAY 47

Victory in the Garden of Agony

"His sweat became like great drops of blood falling down
on the ground."
— Luke 22:44 WEB

Oh Jesus, Redeemer of my soul, You sweat blood so I wouldn't have
to wrestle alone in the dark. You carried the agony of spiritual
warfare to secure my victory before the battle even began. I plead
that blood over every place in my life that feels overwhelmed and
weary.

When I am pressed, Your blood empowers. When my soul is heavy,
Your blood lifts the weight. Let the covering of Your bloody sweat
shield my mind from collapse, my emotions from torment, and my
spirit from fainting in the fight.

I release this prayer over my family. Let none of us give in to the
crushing weight of warfare. The blood has already conquered it. The
same blood that soaked the ground in Gethsemane now covers our
ground of struggle and turns it into holy territory.

We shall not break down—we shall break through. Let the power
in Your agony become the peace in our storm. In Jesus' name,
Amen.

DAY 48

Permanent Deliverance by the Blood

"...through his own blood, entered in once for all into the
Holy Place, having obtained eternal redemption."
— Hebrews 9:12 WEB

Lamb of God, thank You for the once-and-for-all sacrifice that
cannot be reversed. I proclaim the power of eternal redemption
over my life and over every member of my household. Your blood
doesn't expire—it anchors us forever in freedom.

I apply this eternal blood to every lingering chain, every oppressive
pattern, and every generational curse. What the enemy says is
permanent, Your blood declares undone. My deliverance isn't
temporary—it's sealed by heaven's decree.

I will not revisit former bondage. My children will not repeat
ancestral mistakes. My family walks in the permanence of
redemption. No demon, no decision, no delay can reverse what
Your blood has settled.

Thank You, Jesus, for the power of a redemption that lasts forever.
We are delivered, we are secured, and we are Yours. In Jesus' name,
Amen.

DAY 49

THE KING IN BLOOD-SOAKED GLORY

"He is clothed in a garment sprinkled with blood. His name is called 'The Word of God.'"
— Revelation 19:13 WEB

King of Glory, I worship You—mighty in battle, glorious in apparel, and triumphant in blood-soaked splendor. Your victory is not stained—it is royal, righteous, and red with power. I stand under the authority of the Word made flesh and the blood You wore into battle.

Jesus, You are my banner in every war. I call upon Your kingship to reign in my home, to rule over every storm, and to silence every dark voice that would oppose us. You don't fight in theory—you fought in blood and You won in glory.

Let this same blood-drenched authority protect my household. Let it wrap around my children, my spouse, my future, and my legacy. May every plan of the enemy shatter under the force of Your victory.

We declare: our King reigns, clothed in blood, undefeated and eternal. The One who wears the Word and wields the sword is our covering. In Jesus' name, Amen.

DAY 50

FIRE-WALLED BY THE BLOOD

"For I, says Yahweh, will be her wall of fire around her, and
I will be the glory in the middle of her."
— Zechariah 2:5 WEB

O Lord, my Consuming Fire, I stand in awe that You Yourself have
become a fiery wall around my life. Let the blood of Jesus ignite this
wall and make it impenetrable. I decree that every demonic arrow
is burned before it can cross into our space.

Surround my family with fire. Let every window and door in the
spirit be sealed by the flames of Your holiness. Let angelic sentries
guard our perimeter and the glory of Your presence dwell at our
center.

Inside this blood-covered firewall, no fear can thrive, no sickness
can spread, and no plot can prosper. We live within divine
boundaries, invisible to man but known and feared by darkness.

Thank You, Father, that the fire never fades and the blood never
weakens. Our home is protected. Our destiny is preserved. You, O
God, are our flaming fortress. In Jesus' name, Amen.

DAY 51

KEPT FROM ALL HARM

"Yahweh will keep you from all evil. He will keep your soul."
—Psalm 121:7 WEB

O Mighty Keeper of Israel, I boldly declare that You who never sleep nor slumber are the Guardian of my life and the Defender of my family. By the covenant of the blood of Jesus, I claim divine immunity from all forms of evil—visible or invisible, known or unknown. Let the power in the blood serve as our barrier, our defense, our refuge. No arrow that flies by day nor pestilence that stalks at night shall come near us.

Father, keep us secure in every journey we take, in every step we make, in every room we enter, and in every relationship we engage. Let the blood of Jesus speak louder than every trap, lie, ambush, or assignment of darkness. Day and night, let Your eyes watch over us and Your angels encamp around us, enforcing the covenant that covers our household in supernatural safety.

Lord, You are our Keeper, our Shade, our Fortress, and our Shield. We are hidden in Christ, above the reach of harm and beyond the limits of natural protection. By the blood, we abide in divine preservation. No weapon formed against us shall prosper, and no evil shall befall us. We walk covered, sealed, and secured—every hour, every moment.

In Jesus' name, Amen.

DAY 52

Marked With Christ's Ownership

"From now on, let no one cause me any trouble, for I bear
the marks of the Lord Jesus branded on my body."
—Galatians 6:17 WEB

Righteous Redeemer, I stand boldly under the eternal mark of the
Lord Jesus Christ. The blood that was shed for me is a permanent
sign of divine ownership. I am not my own. My family is not
unclaimed. We are marked, labeled, and sealed by heaven's
decree—set apart for Your glory, untouchable by the forces of
darkness.

Let the blood-mark be visible in the spirit realm, announcing to
every evil force that we belong to the Lord Most High. Let every
demonic agenda break and shatter at the sight of this covenant
mark. Our ears are tuned to heaven, our steps ordered by
righteousness, our hands cleansed for holy service. Nothing
unclean, cursed, or diabolical can stick to our lives or lay hold of
our destiny.

Lord, when the enemy surveys for an open door, let him see only
the blood. When trouble searches for a landing place, let it pass over
us. We are covered, stamped, and branded with the authority of
Jesus Christ. Let this mark speak for us in moments of battle,
temptation, and judgment. We are blood-marked and spiritually
guarded.

In Jesus' name, Amen.

DAY 53

REDEEMED AND HIDDEN BY BLOOD

"These are those who were not defiled... These were redeemed from among men to be first fruits to God and to the Lamb."
—Revelation 14:4 WEB

Precious Lamb of God, I thank You for redeeming me by Your holy blood. My name is written in the Lamb's Book of Life, and my identity is sealed in Your sacrifice. I declare that I and my household are the redeemed of the Lord, separated from destruction and exempted from the curses of this world. We are not common—we are consecrated.

Let the blood declare our distinction wherever we go. When judgment passes, let us be hidden. When calamity rages, let us be sheltered. When systems collapse and hearts fail, let our redemption speak deliverance. We are not of this world; we are ambassadors, a royal priesthood, a protected inheritance in Christ. Let our lives bear the fruit of Your ownership—purity, power, and protection.

Father, redeem every area of our lives that has been under bondage. Let every family chain be broken, every soul tie severed, every generational pattern reversed. We stand as the purchased ones—redeemed, secured, and forever sheltered under the covenant of Your blood.

In Jesus' name, Amen.

DAY 54

COVERED BY DIVINE SURVEILLANCE

"As birds hovering, so Yahweh of Armies will protect Jerusalem. He will protect and deliver it. He will pass over and preserve it."
—Isaiah 31:5 WEB

Lord of Hosts, I thank You that You hover over my home like an eagle over its young, never blinking, never retreating. By the blood of Jesus, I activate the supernatural surveillance system of heaven. Day and night, You scan the perimeters of my life, detecting threats before they arise and intercepting every arrow before it lands.

Let the eyes of the Lord shine around my household. Let the fire of divine presence be upon our walls and in our gates. Every unseen enemy, every silent danger, every coded curse—expose and destroy it, O God. Let the blood of Jesus function as an alarm system that cannot be hacked or disabled.

Father, I declare that nothing escapes Your attention—not even the smallest schemes of the enemy. You will protect, You will deliver, You will pass over and preserve. Your watchful care is our constant safety. Because of the blood, we do not fear the ambush. We do not fear the night. We are under constant divine surveillance.

In Jesus' name, Amen.

DAY 55

JESUS KEEPS WHAT'S ENTRUSTED

"While I was with them in the world, I kept them in your name. Those whom you have given me I have kept."
—John 17:12 WEB

Holy Shepherd and Guardian of my soul, I praise You for keeping power. I entrust my life and the lives of my loved ones into Your nail-scarred hands. Your blood is not only our covering—it is our keeping. You are faithful to guard what has been given into Your hands. Let no one be lost, no one snatched, no one broken beyond repair.

Lord, I declare that my children, my marriage, my calling, my destiny—all are kept by Your blood. No demonic snare, no worldly enticement, no spiritual decay will prevail against the ones You have claimed. Let Your blood seal every door against backsliding and despair. Let Your voice keep us from deception and danger.

Even when we walk through the fire, we will not be consumed. When we pass through the waters, we will not drown. Because You are with us, and Your blood has marked us, we are preserved, protected, and pursued by divine mercy. Jesus, You keep what the Father gives—and we are safe in You.

In Jesus' name, Amen.

DAY 56

SHIELDED FROM END-TIME CALAMITY

"Because you kept my command to endure, I also will keep you from the hour of testing…"
—Revelation 3:10 WEB

Almighty God, in a world shaking with chaos, I take refuge in the blood of Jesus, my eternal Passover. You promised to keep those who endure in faith from the hour of great trial. I plead the blood over my family and all we possess. Let the blood build a wall of preservation in days of disaster, and let divine endurance anchor our hearts in peace.

Father, shield us from the judgments that fall on rebellion. Let our obedience place us under divine exemption. The blood cries louder than any plague or famine. When economies fail and nations tremble, let our covenant stand as our safety net. Let us be as Goshen was in Egypt—lit while others are in darkness, protected while others are struck.

Lord, You are not only our Savior, but our Shelter in the storm. Let every global shaking only deepen our security in You. We are marked, sealed, and hidden from wrath through the precious blood of the Lamb.

In Jesus' name, Amen.

DAY 57

GUARDED FROM SATANIC AMBUSH

"But the Lord is faithful, who will establish you and guard
you from the evil one."
—2 Thessalonians 3:3 WEB

Faithful God, I lift my voice and decree: No ambush, trap, or
demonic scheme will prevail against me or my family. For the Lord
is our strong tower, and the blood of Jesus is our impenetrable
fortress. Let every plan of the enemy fail before it begins. Let every
snare be revealed and overturned before we step into it.

Lord, establish our feet on holy ground. Let the blood neutralize
every spiritual surveillance and demonic tracking. Frustrate the
enemy's blueprints, intercept his whispers, and dismantle his
weapons. We are guarded not by flesh, but by the faithfulness of a
covenant-keeping God whose blood speaks louder than our fears.

Strengthen us in the inner man, and let divine discernment sharpen
our senses. We declare: No premature death, no tragic event, no
satanic manipulation will take root in our lives. The evil one cannot
touch what the blood has secured. Guard our minds, our health,
our homes, and our lineage.

In Jesus' name, Amen.

DAY 58

STANDARD AGAINST FLOOD ATTACKS

"So shall they fear Yahweh's name from the west, and his glory from the rising of the sun; for when the enemy comes in like a flood, Yahweh's Spirit will lift up a standard against him."
—Isaiah 59:19 WEB

God of Battle, I raise the banner of the blood high over my household. When the enemy rushes in like a flood—through fear, through chaos, through sudden assault—let the blood of Jesus rise as a standard. Let it be a wall he cannot penetrate, a floodgate he cannot breach.

I decree that my family will not drown in emotional overload, spiritual weariness, or financial pressure. When trials increase, Your glory increases all the more. The blood stands as proof that the enemy's access is denied. Let every flood meant to overwhelm be turned into a wave of breakthrough.

Father, make our dwelling a high place—above floodwaters, above panic, above demonic manipulation. The blood of Jesus is our high tower. When the enemy overreaches, You overrule. Raise up angels to fight on our behalf, raise up favor to counter attack, raise up victory to cancel sorrow.

In Jesus' name, Amen.

DAY 59

Shielded by God Himself

"But you, Yahweh, are a shield around me, my glory, and
the one who lifts up my head."
—Psalm 3:3 WEB

O Shield of My Life, I declare that You are not only near me—you
are around me. Encircle my family like fire. Surround my home like
wind. Let the blood of Jesus form an unbreakable circumference of
protection, so that no harm can penetrate.

Be our glory when shame tries to creep in. Be our lifter when heads
hang low. I speak over every member of my household: The Lord is
your shield! You are surrounded with favor, soaked in mercy, and
defended by divine fire. Nothing formed against us shall stand.

Lord, as we go out and come in, let the shield of Your presence go
before us. Let it block what we don't see and destroy what we can't
hear. Let every ambush dissolve before it manifests. We rest tonight
and rise tomorrow with heads lifted high—not by our strength, but
because of the shield of the blood.

In Jesus' name, Amen.

DAY 60

THE BLOOD, MY STRONGHOLD

"Yahweh is good, a stronghold in the day of trouble; he
knows those who take refuge in him."
—Nahum 1:7 WEB

Rock of Ages, I run into You, my stronghold in every storm. I
declare that the blood of Jesus is not only my shelter—it is my
spiritual bunker. When trouble rages and threats multiply, I will not
fear. You know my name. You know my voice. You know my family.
We are known and covered by the blood.

Lord, let every day of trouble meet the power of the blood. Let every
dark forecast be reversed by divine goodness. Raise up walls around
us made not of stone, but of Your promises. Let our home be a
fortress where peace rules, angels dwell, and deliverance is
standard.

When the winds howl and the earth shakes, we will not be moved.
We dwell in the secret place of the Most High. The blood has
spoken: We are not forsaken. We are fortified. We are hidden. We
are loved. And the Lord is our stronghold, forever faithful.

In Jesus' name, Amen.

EPILOGUE

Still Covered. Forever Shielded.

You've reached the end of this 60-day journey—but you've only just begun to live under the full power of Christ's blood. The truths you've prayed, the Scriptures you've declared, and the spiritual principles you've absorbed are not temporary—they are eternal. The blood of Jesus is not seasonal protection; it is an everlasting covenant that still speaks better things than the blood of Abel (Hebrews 12:24).

You may not have seen every outward battle end, but something has shifted in the spirit. You have drawn a bloodline around your life. The enemy knows it. Heaven knows it. And now, so do you.

Now walk in it.

Do not let fear return to your thoughts or doors. Do not allow passivity to creep in. Remain vigilant. Make the application of the blood a lifestyle. Cover your home before you sleep. Plead the blood over your children before they step out. Declare your blood covenant before signing contracts, making decisions, or engaging spiritual warfare.

This has been more than a devotional—it's been divine training ground. You've been equipped. Keep the sword in your hand and the covering over your life. You are not a victim; you are a covenant child. You are not merely protected; you are positioned in Christ, hidden in God.

As you move forward, speak the truth boldly: *"I live under the blood. I stand untouchable. My life is divinely shielded."*

Remain sealed, remain secure, and remain strong.

In Jesus' name, Amen.

ENCOURAGE OTHERS WITH YOUR STORY

If this prayer guide has strengthened your faith, deepened your intercession, or helped you stand in the gap, would you consider leaving a short review on Amazon? Your feedback not only encourages others but also helps more believers discover this resource and join in the prayer movement. Every review—just a few sentences—makes a difference. Thank you for being part of this movement.

PARDON THROUGH THE BLOOD:

60 DAYS OF PRAYERS FOR TOTAL FORGIVENESS AND FREEDOM

Guilt is a prison. The blood of Jesus holds the key.

Pardon Through the Blood invites you on a 60-day journey into the liberating power of Christ's sacrifice—a sacred cleansing that reaches deeper than shame, regret, or condemnation. If you've ever felt stuck in cycles of failure, haunted by your past, or burdened by hidden sin, this book is your roadmap to lasting forgiveness and spiritual freedom. Each day offers a blood-specific Scripture, a focused prayer theme, and a prophetic, Spirit-filled prayer that will help you boldly approach God's mercy seat. You'll experience what it means to be fully forgiven, deeply cleansed, and restored to right relationship with the Father—all through the blood of Jesus.

PREVAIL THROUGH THE BLOOD:

60 DAYS OF PRAYERS FOR SPIRITUAL MASTERY OVER THE ENEMY

What if every scheme of the enemy against your life could be dismantled—by one unstoppable weapon?

In *Prevail Through the Blood*, you'll discover how to wield the most powerful force in the universe—the Blood of Jesus Christ—to overcome every spiritual assault, shatter generational yokes, and walk in daily victory. This is more than a prayer book. It is your 60-day spiritual war manual, designed to train your hands for battle and your heart for triumph. This third installment in The Blood Covenant Series invites you into a journey of spiritual mastery. Whether you are in the heat of battle or standing in victory, every page will sharpen your discernment, stir your faith, and saturate your home in the protective power of Christ's blood.

Break free from every chain. Pray with fire. Win with the Blood.

PRESERVATION THROUGH THE BLOOD:

60 DAYS OF PRAYERS FOR DIVINE HEALING AND WHOLENESS

Unlock Lasting Healing and Wholeness Through the Blood of Jesus

Preservation Through the Blood: 60 Days of Prayers for Divine Healing and Wholeness is your prophetic, Scripture-packed guide to receiving total restoration in your body, soul, and spirit through the covenant power of Christ's blood. More than a devotional, this book is a healing altar—built on 60 carefully selected Bible verses that directly reveal God's will to heal and preserve you.

Whether you're battling chronic illness, emotional trauma, lingering symptoms, or generational afflictions, these blood-based prayers will speak directly to the root of the issue to appropriate divine healing. This book equips you to confront the source, not just the symptoms.

PROSPERITY THROUGH THE BLOOD:

60 DAYS OF PRAYERS FOR UNLOCKING HEAVEN'S WEALTH AND WALKING IN COVENANT INCREASE

You were redeemed for more than survival—
you were redeemed to prosper.

In a world filled with economic uncertainty, God's promise of abundance still stands. *Prosperity Through the Blood: 60 Days of Prayers for Unlocking Heaven's Wealth and Walking in Covenant Increase* invites you into a powerful journey of discovering what the blood of Jesus truly purchased for you—not just eternal life, but a full, flourishing, and prosperous life on earth. Whether you're in a season of financial need or simply hungry to experience more of what belongs to you in Christ, *Prosperity Through the Blood* is your roadmap to living untouchable, unshakable, and abundantly blessed under the power of the blood.

PEACE THROUGH THE BLOOD:

60 Days of Prayers for Resting in the Covenant of Unshakable Peace

Are you ready to silence every storm of the mind, heart, and home—once and for all?

Peace is not the absence of problems—it is the presence of Christ Himself. And through the blood of His cross, that peace has already been purchased, sealed, and placed into your covenant inheritance. You don't have to fight for it—you only have to receive and enforce it.

This book is your daily guide to experiencing heaven's calm in every circumstance. Rooted in Colossians 1:20—"having made peace through the blood of his cross"—this book will lead you into prophetic, Scripture-anchored prayers that confront anxiety, heal emotional wounds, restore fractured relationships, and anchor your soul in God's unshakable rest.

COMMAND YOUR MORNING: 30 DAYS OF PRAYERS AND DECLARATIONS TO SEIZE YOUR DAY AND SHAPE YOUR DESTINY

There is a battle over every morning—and every believer must choose to either drift into the day or command it.

Command Your Morning: 30 Days of Prayers and Declarations to Seize Your Day and Shape Your Destiny is a spiritually charged guide to help you start each day with purpose, power, and prophetic clarity. This is more than a devotional—it's a call to action. Each day in this 30-day journey is built around **five core biblical themes** that set the spiritual tone for your day: **Praise, Purpose, Protection, Provision** and **Position**. Don't just wake up. Command your morning—and shape your destiny.

COMMAND YOUR NIGHT: 30 DAYS OF PRAYERS AND DECLARATIONS TO SECURE YOUR REST AND SHAPE YOUR TOMORROW

Every night is a spiritual battlefield—what you do before you sleep can determine the course of your tomorrow.

Command Your Night: 30 Days of Prayers and Declarations to Secure Your Rest and Shape Your Tomorrow is a powerful devotional prayer manual designed to help you end each day in victory, not vulnerability. Whether you're battling anxiety, spiritual attacks, restlessness, or simply longing for deeper peace, this book equips you to reclaim your night with bold, Scripture-rooted prayers. Each night is structured around five strategic prayer themes: *Shut, Shield, Silence, Show, Sleep.*

COMMAND YOUR EVENING: 30 DAYS OF PRAYERS AND DECLARATIONS TO RELEASE THE DAY AND RECLAIM INTIMACY WITH GOD

There is a battle over every transition—and evening is one of the most spiritually neglected.

Command Your Evening is the third book in the **Command Your Destiny** series—following *Command Your Morning* and *Command Your Night*. In heaven's rhythm, the evening is not just a wind-down—it's a window. A sacred hour where destinies are recalibrated, burdens are lifted, and hearts are re-centered in the presence of God. In *Command Your Evening*, you'll journey through 30 days of intentional, Spirit-led prayers and prophetic declarations centered around five key evening themes: **Release, Renew, Refocus, Rebuild,** and **Rest.**

SCRIPTURES & PRAYERS FOR DELIVERANCE FROM TROUBLE:

40 DAYS OF PRAYER FOR WHEN LIFE FEELS OVERWHELMING

Are you walking through a season where life feels heavy, hope feels distant, and your prayers feel weak?

Scriptures & Prayers for Deliverance from Trouble is a 40-day journey of honest prayers and powerful Scriptures to help you find peace, strength, and healing when life is overwhelming. Each day offers a personal, Scripture-based prayer written in the language of real faith and raw trust. This devotional isn't about perfect words— it's about real connection with God when you need Him most.

Scriptures & Prayers for Deliverance from Evil:

50 Days of Prayer to Overcome Darkness and Find God's Protection

---

When darkness presses in, how do you pray?

When fear grips your heart or unseen battles rage around you, you need more than generic words—you need Scripture, truth, and the steady hand of God to lead you through.

Scriptures & Prayers for Deliverance from Evil: 50 Days of Prayer to Overcome Darkness and Find God's Protection is a powerful devotional journey designed to help you pray boldly and biblically through seasons of spiritual warfare, oppression, fear, or uncertainty.

SCRIPTURES & PRAYERS FOR ENGAGING THE ENEMY:

70 DAYS OF PRAYER TO REBUKE THE ENEMY AND RELEASE GOD'S POWER

You weren't called to run from the battle—

you were anointed to win it.

Scriptures & Prayers for Engaging the Enemy: 70 Days of Prayer to Rebuke the Enemy and Release God's Power is a bold devotional for believers who are ready to rise, resist, and reclaim what the enemy has tried to steal. If you're tired of feeling spiritually outnumbered, this book will equip you to fight back—with Scripture in your mouth and power in your prayers. Over 70 days, you'll be guided through five strategic phases of spiritual warfare: (1) Rebuking the Enemy, (2) Releasing Terror Upon the Enemy (3) Praying for the Fall of the Enemy (4) Treading Upon the Enemy (5) When Heaven Strikes.

The war is real. But so is your victory.

SCRIPTURES & PRAYERS FOR COMBATING SPIRITUAL WICKEDNESS:

50 DAYS OF PRAYER TO OVERTHROW WICKED PLANS AND STAND IN GOD'S VICTORY

Are you facing opposition that feels deeper than the natural? Do you sense hidden resistance working against your progress, peace, or purpose? You're not imagining it—and you're not powerless.

Rooted in the authority of Scripture and fueled by bold, targeted prayers, *Scriptures & Prayers for Combating Spiritual Wickedness* equips you to confront darkness head-on. Each day features a focused Bible passage and a heartfelt, Scripture-based prayer designed to nullify ungodly counsel, disrupt demonic schemes, and establish God's victory in every area of your life.

STANDING IN THE GAP FOR COVENANT AWAKENING:

30 DAYS OF PRAYER FOR NATIONAL REPENTANCE, RIGHTEOUS LEADERSHIP & GOD'S SOVEREIGN RULE

What if your prayers could help turn the tide of a nation?

America stands at a spiritual crossroads. Division deepens, truth is under siege, and righteousness is being redefined. But God is still searching for those who will stand in the gap—intercessors who will cry out for mercy, justice, and national awakening.

Standing in the Gap for Covenant Awakening is a 30-day prayer guide for believers who sense the urgency of the hour and long to see their nation return to God.

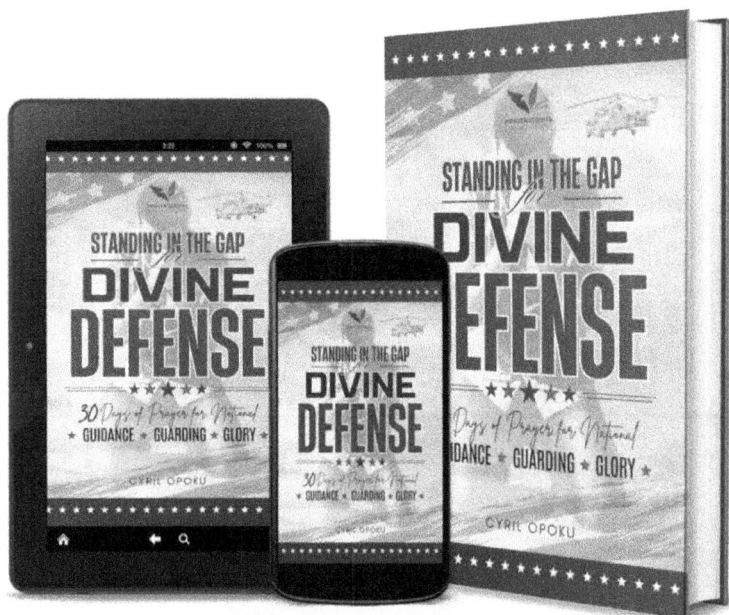

STANDING IN THE GAP FOR DIVINE DEFENSE:

30 DAYS OF PRAYER FOR NATIONAL GUIDANCE, GUARDING & GLORY

When the foundations of a nation feel as if they're shaking, prayer is the strongest fortress you can build.

Standing in the Gap for Divine Defense: 30 Days of Prayer for National Guidance, Guarding & Glory is your call to action—a 30-day journey of powerful, Scripture-rooted intercession that invites everyday believers to become watchmen on the walls for their nation. Drawing on timeless truths from God's Word, this devotional equips you to stand in the gap for your nation and **Seek Heaven's Wisdom, Secure Divine Protection,** and **Ignite Spiritual Awakening.** If you sense the urgency of the hour and long to see your country guided and guarded by the hand of God, open these pages. Stand in the gap. Watch Him move.

STANDING IN THE GAP FOR NATIONAL HEALING:

40 DAYS OF PRAYER FOR RECONCILIATION, RIGHTEOUSNESS, AND RESTORATION

What if your prayers could help heal a nation? What if God is waiting for someone—like you—to stand in the gap?

Standing in the Gap for National Healing: 40 Days of Prayer for Reconciliation, Righteousness, and Restoration is a bold, Spirit-filled call to action for believers who refuse to sit on the sidelines while their nation drifts further from God. In a time marked by division, confusion, and moral decline, this book equips you to pray with power, precision, and unshakable hope. Inside, you'll find 40 days of Scripture-based intercession divided into three strategic sections: **Peace, Unity & Reconciliation, Morality, Truth & Righteous Leadership**, and **National Restoration & Reformation**. It's time to stop watching history unfold—and start shaping it in prayer.

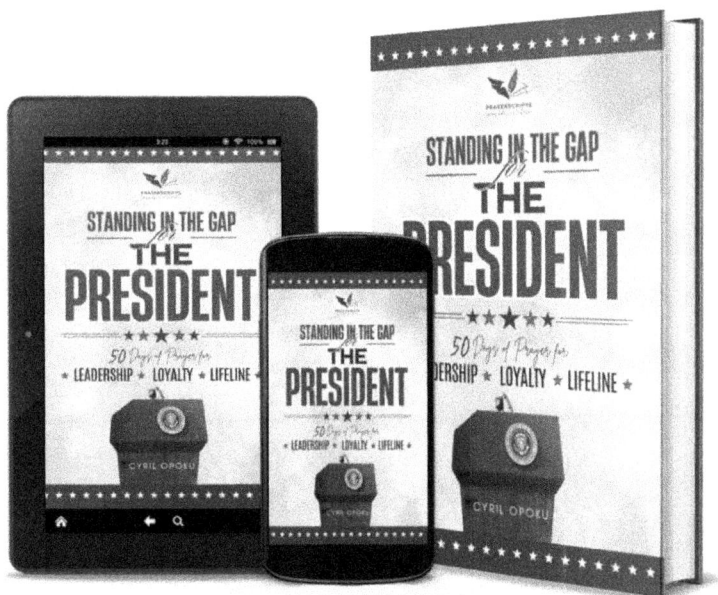

STANDING IN THE GAP FOR THE PRESIDENT:

50 DAYS OF PRAYER FOR LEADERSHIP, LOYALTY, AND LIFELINE

When a nation's leader is under spiritual siege, will you answer the call to stand in the gap?

Standing in the Gap for The President: 50 Days of Prayer for Leadership, Loyalty, and Lifeline is a bold, Scripture-saturated prayer guide for those who understand that the battles facing our leaders are more than political—they are spiritual. Assassination attempts, betrayal from within, and attacks on character and conscience are not just headlines—they're signs of the times. Inside, you'll find 50 days of strategic intercession divided into three high-impact sections: **Presidential Character & Leadership**, **Against Disloyal Insiders**, and **Against Assassination Attempts**. The future of a nation can shift through the prayers of the faithful. It's time to stand in the gap.

www.ingramcontent.com/pod-product-compliance
Lightning Source LLC
Chambersburg PA
CBHW062020040426
42447CB00010B/2084